7 Ways To Make Money For Kids

Teaching Kids Money Management, Practical Money Skills And How To Think About Money

Frank Dixon

Before we begin, I have something special waiting for you. An action-packed 1 page printout with a few quick & easy tips taken from this book that you can start using today to become a better parent right now!

It's my gift to you, free of cost. Think of it as my way of saying thank you to you for purchasing this book.

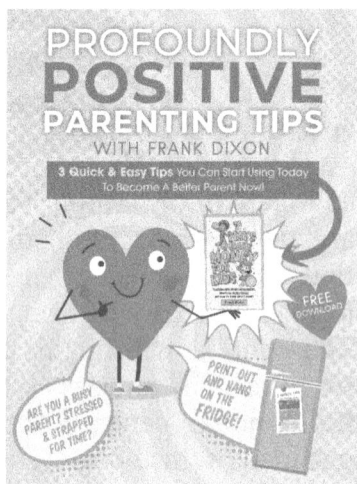

Claim your download of Profoundly Positive Parenting with Frank Dixon by scanning the QR code below and join my mailing list.

Sign up below to grab your free copy, print it out and hang it on the fridge!

Sign Up By Scanning The QR Code With Your Phone's Camera To Be Redirected To A Page To Enter Your Email And Receive INSTANT Access To Your Download

Before we jump in, I'd like to express my gratitude. I know this mustn't be the first book you came across and yet you still decided to give it a read. There are numerous courses and guides you could have picked instead that promise to make you an ideal and well-rounded parent while raising your children to be the best they can be.

But for some reason, mine stood out from the rest and this makes me the happiest person on the planet right now. If you stick with it, I promise this will be a worthwhile read.

In the pages that follow, you're going to learn the best parenting skills so that your child can grow to become the best version of themselves and in doing so experience a meaningful understanding of what it means to be an effective parent.

Notable Quotes About Parenting

"Children Must Be Taught How To Think, Not What To Think."

— Margaret Mead

"It's easier to build strong children than to fix broken men [or women]."

- Frederick Douglass

"Truly great friends are hard to find, difficult to leave, and impossible to forget."

— George Randolf

"Nothing in life is to be feared, it is only to be understood. Now is the time to understand more, so that we may fear less."

— Scientist Marie Curie

Table of Contents

Introduction

From the moment they are born, children begin to develop behavioral habits. They will have different sleeping patterns, act cranky when bored, hungry, or have pooped. When they get a little older, their habits and behaviors will once again change over time and then again as they start school.

Their spending habits are no different than their daily habits. Their sentiment about money plays a crucial role in their financial future and therefore, it is best to start early. They notice how you handle your finances and look up to you for guidance. They look at how their friends at school handle their lunch money and take mental notes. They see their elder sibling or relative spending on luxuries and they take a hint there, too. They develop a relationship with money as their concepts involving finances become clearer and more solid.

Teaching them to create positive relationships with money in a way that they see as an asset and value, is important. Habits are like a pearl necklace. Each day we weave in another pearl. With every new pearl in it, it becomes stronger and harder to break. Financial habits can be good and bad too. Some kids don't value money because they have a lot of it while others have to work for it by taking jobs during the holidays. When we, their parents, inculcate good financial habits at a young age, we can raise them to become financially independent and responsible adults. They should know about the benefits of saving and the perks of delayed spending. They should know the difference between a need and a want and not overspend their allowance. They should know what items or areas of spending are worth it and what aren't. They should know that borrowing from others has consequences and learn to cut down their expenses so that they don't have to reach out to others.

Financial literacy doesn't mean that your child should know how to sign off checks or contracts before they are five. It means that they must develop the ability to use their skills and knowledge about money to make effective and informed decisions. They shouldn't just know how to earn money or get a side gig going, they should also know how to manage it and invest it in profitable stakes.

A lot of parents, when inquired if they have talked about financial literacy with their kids, respond with the same answer: aren't they too young? Truth be told, a child aged three starts to understand the concept of spending and saving. They may not have all the concepts developed super clearly but they do understand that money can get them what they want. Early positive experiences around finances will help a child shape their preferences, behaviors, and attitudes. By the time they reach the age of seven, their money habits have typically been set. If you don't introduce them to positive money habits during this phase, it will be challenging for them to handle money matters efficiently later on.

While schools focus more on familiarizing children with traditional academic topics, not much importance is given to subjects like finance or economics. As a result, children haven't sufficiently developed the concepts of money's worth, saving, and spending. The only source they can turn to is your guidance and if you fail to provide it, it can be laborious to do even basic calculations in the future.

Teaching children about financial literacy early on and consistently throughout their academic career has many tangible benefits. According to Annamaria Lusardi, an economic and accountancy professor, what if our children knew to put money in their 401k the day they start their first job (Lusardi & Mitchell, 2014)? What if they learn to save from the young age of 20 and not 50? Wouldn't that take off a ton of stress from their lives? Wouldn't they feel financially stable and independent? She further believes that parents and educators don't have to sit down children to teach them money; they can integrate the ideas and basic concepts in existing lessons and life experiences so that they don't feel overwhelmed.

Following her advice, this guide is going to be about teaching kids how to make money, manage it, and spend it wisely. It will look at several money-generating avenues that young kids can explore and earn their first paycheck. It will help you, as their parents, to guide them about how to be wise with their pocket money, introduce to them the ideas and benefits of savings, and present the concept of investing so that they can feel in control and make better choices when it comes to spending what little they have.

Kids and teenagers who lack financial literacy can have a hard time comprehending investments, loans, interest rates, or budgeting. Financial literacy empowers them and helps them create a relaxed, yet meaningful life. When they are aware of the importance of good credit scores, different types of investments, and how interest rates work, they will remain vigilant and careful about what they spend on.

It will also prevent overspending. Overspending in youth can ruin one's financial stability long in the future, thus, they must know how to prioritize their needs from a young age and spend only on their needs and not on wants. It will motivate them to save for a rainy day and have an emergency fund so that they can cope with unexpected circumstances without having to add the burden of debt on their shoulders.

We'll start from the very basics and dive right into the early developmental stages of children and how they view money. By the time you are done reading this, you will be convinced to begin healthy financial discussions at home without delay.

Chapter 1:

An Age-Appropriate Guide to Teaching Kids About Money

According to Dan Kadlec, a contributor to Time Magazine, young people need to be taught the basics of finances. With the ever-growing demand for freedom and independence in youngsters, knowing how to manage their finances should be their top priority (Kadlec, 2014). If they want to live by their means, they must know how to. This starts with understanding the basics of monetary transactions and where to invest or spend them. Although many smart apps help kids get their money sorted, as parents, it is still our job to get things in motion.

As they are the digital natives—the future of tomorrow—it is time to impart our tried and true financial wisdom and combine it with modern solutions like online payments so that they know how to survive, earn, and thrive in a world that is going cashless.

Author Jayne A. Pearl argues that it is fairly easy to teach kids about money. All parents have to do is turn day-to-day activities into learning experiences (Pearl, 1999). For example, if you are going out shopping, encourage them to pay attention when you are paying the cashier. If you are at the bank with them, show them how to use an ATM or if they are older, encourage them to give it a try on their own. If they are young, even a simple trip to the bank or the store will get the conversation started. You can also include basic money concepts in their imaginary games or invest in toys like a pretend cash register toy to get them interested in talking money.

A lot of parents question when the right time to have money conversations with their kids is, and this is exactly what we are going to explore in this first chapter. Not only that, we are going to discuss what to talk to them about and at which age and what concepts they should be aware of at different developmental milestones. Keeping it action-oriented to help you get the most benefit, each section also explores some of the best games, activities, and suggestions on how to get through to your children, regardless of their age, to become financially literate.

Toddlers

Kids aged one and above don't have a clear idea about spending but they do know that money gets them stuff.

They watch you giving it away when you stop at a gas station or shop for groceries. At this stage, kids are more interested in collecting coins than paper money. They think coins are more valuable because they are heavier and in a larger amount. They feel real and they can slide them into their piggy banks. They have a basic idea of counting and therefore, can count the quantities of money (coin/paper) they have.

Activities

This is a great time to teach them how to add coins to form a value. For example, you can teach them that ten dimes make $1. Similarly, you can engage them in plays that include money like a pretend restaurant or café where they act as the waiter and you pay them at the end of the meal or vice versa. Encourage them to pay cash with their own hands because it helps them form an immediate connection.

You can also play memory-building games where you ask them to remember the names of different coins and solve basic math questions using them.

Another interesting game is to trace the coins on a piece of paper and then ask your toddler to match them with the ones they have in their piggy bank. We call this the coin identification game. This way, they will learn the names of the coins too.

You can also create a pretend play store where you act as a customer and they act as a cashier and you buy things and offer cash in return. This will teach them that goods are earned via money and hopefully, they will stop trying to steal or put things in their bag when out shopping (if they have developed the habit of it).

Kindergartners and Elementary Students

By now, kids know that they need money to buy something. By the time they are six or seven, they have developed basic financial behaviors. If not, you can help them by ditching your credit card at home and pay using cold hard cash when shopping with them. You can encourage them to count before paying someone and teach them how different kinds of coins and bills can be grouped. Some days, your kindergartner will want to have the money as well as what they intended to buy from it. They might not want to give it up. This is the time when you must tell them that to get something, they have to spend it—aka: let it go. Tell them that they can only spend it once so they must be careful as to where they spend it.

To encourage exchange and spending, give them a dollar when out shopping and tell them that they can use it to get something they want but it must cost less than one dollar. Once they select, they must hand over the dollar to the cashier to get the item of their choice.

At this stage, they should also have the basic idea of earning. If you give them allowance for completing simple chores, ensure that the allowance is only given after they have finished the chore so they know that it is a reward for their hard work. This will instill the concept of earning. They will know that they will have to earn their allowance by working hard or they don't get paid.

You should also try to empower them to use their money responsibly. They might be a little young to differentiate between a need and a want but it is never too soon to begin. They should know that the money they have earned must be spent wisely as opposed to the money they receive as a present or a bonus. Once they buy something using their money, ensure that it belongs solely to them. They will feel like they have earned it.

Now is also a good time to talk about savings. As they begin to earn their allowances, let them know that they can choose to save them and put them away. Tell them that different things come at a different price and if they wish to buy something expensive like a new game for themselves, then they must save what they have. If they seem impatient, ask them if they would like to add some bonus allowance by working some extra chores.

Activities

An ideal game to get your child to save and spend their money wisely is by giving them a saving jar. Although having a piggy bank is no different than a jar, the goal is to give the child a visual and teach delayed gratification. Seeing the jar every day, filling up with their daily pocket money, will tempt them. If they learn to resist, they will learn about responsibility. If they can't resist, they will learn the lesson of being unwise by spending it on things that are temporary attractions. Also, when they see the jar filling up in front of them, they can see their money grow. Not only is it a great feeling for young ones, but it also cultivates a constructive saving habit.

Be practical. You don't have to sit down and lecture them about financial literacy. Teach them through experiences. For example, every time you are going out for something, ask them to grab some money from your wallet. Be specific about how much you need. Meaning, don't just tell them to get $5, tell them to get $5, 5 dimes, and 25 cents. They will then have to be more careful and vigilant and learn to add and subtract too.

Middle Schoolers

Having grasped the basic concepts well, your grade-schooler now wants to learn more. Now that they are around ten or eleven, it is time to teach them about opportunity costs, how they can get a side gig and earn money, and how they can save it, in detail. Chances are, they are already spending on things they like and understand how much is required to get something.

They know that once they have given away the money in exchange for something, it is spent.

Talking to them about opportunity costs is important. It helps them make efficient decisions. They must know that if they choose to buy a DVD from their saved money, they will have to wait to get that pair of shoes they have been wanting for so long. Let them decide what matters more. Ask them to come up with a list of pros and cons for each item under debate and then go with the one with the most use and urgency. Either way, they will have to live with the decision they made and the possible outcome.

Next, introduce different types of spending options so they gain a better understanding of where to spend it. For example, you must have the need vs. wants discussion with them. Tell them that although it is okay to go with impulse or emotion and buy something for themselves, this shouldn't become a habit. Needs include essentials like food, milk, stationery, etc. Whereas wants come after a need has been fulfilled. Meaning if you are hungry, any food in the fridge will do to prevent you from starving. However, if you are hungry and you will only agree to eat a granola bar, fruit loops, or a peanut butter jelly sandwich, then those particular desires are a want. You can do without wants but not without a need.

Your child should know the distinction between the two. The best way to teach them this is by asking them to make a list of all the things they would get from the supermarket. Once they create a list, sit down with them, and ask them to differentiate a need from a want. Discuss how some things are *needs* in contrast with more frivolous *wants*. Now ask them to count the money that they have and create a rough estimate of how much all the things under the "need" column would cost. If there is money to spare, ask them to get something from the "want" list.

They should also know about short-term and long-term goals. Teaching them this will help them decide how to spend their money wisely. Again, you can ask them to prepare a list of their short and long-term goals. Then roughly calculate how much they will need to earn and save to accomplish those goals. For example, if one of their short-term goals includes getting selected for their school's basketball team, they will need money for the extra coaching they would require. They might also need a basketball and a basketball net installed at the house, which again, is going to come at a price. Let them know how much it will cost and then help them plan a budget so that they can utilize the saved money to get the basketball and the hoop.

Then, you must also put a stop to impulse buying and lay down the drawbacks of it in front of them. Consider this as an example: Imagine you are at the mall with your child and they insist on getting that cute dress on the mannequin. This age group is known to capitalize on the impulse buy, especially when they can use their parents' money. Stand your ground and let them know that such behavior is unacceptable and if they want something, they must figure out the means to gather the money for it. Suggest doing some extra chores around the house to help them get started and see how things go from there.

Activities

Teach them how to be charitable and present it as a good deed that they must get into the habit of doing. They are big enough to understand how it feels to be poor. They must know how they should hold back on purchases because they didn't have the money or wait before they had enough. Motivate them to help the needy by sharing what they have or by helping them out financially. For example, if you see someone begging around the street, ask your child how they would feel if they help them out. Tell them how giving away just a little bit will make a big difference in their lives.

To encourage supporting charitable causes, make them a promise that for every dollar that they spend helping the poor, you will add two quarters in their savings jar. Tempt them that they can do whatever they can with that money and spend it as they like. Also, research organizations together that help provide housing, food, and clothes. You can take your child there and ask them to give away the money from their hands so that they can feel proud of it and make a connection to the lives they are impacting.

Here is another great activity to teach about the importance of money and why it should be spent wisely: Go to a bakery and let your child get their favorite cake, cookie, or pie—whatever they love the most. On the way home, make a stop at the grocery store and get all the ingredients required to make the same sweet treat you just purchased. Yes, you heard that right. The goal is to teach them how they can bake the same thing for less so that they become wiser on what things to spend their money on. Also, when shopping for separate ingredients, don't just pick the first one you see on the rack. Ask your child to sort through the many substitute bands and see if they can find a cheaper version of the same product. For example, when baking a cake, you don't always have to invest in expensive vanilla extract. You can easily find it among cheaper and lesser-known brands.

Another activity to get them interested in paper money and coins is by asking them to research the people printed on them and why they are there. This will motivate them to research and learn not just about money but many famous people and their lives. A win-win situation for them, if you ask us!

You can also bring them books that teach kids about money management or allow them to play online games that involve handling money. For example, there are many pretend restaurant games where you have to complete daily money goals by preparing food for the customers. You also earn tips that help you upgrade kitchen appliances to lower cooking times. You can easily find them on Google Play or the Apple store.

Teenagers

By this time, they are probably dealing with money on their own and making mostly sensible choices. However, this is also the stage where the puberty hormones kick in and both boys and girls become extra cautious about their reputation and physique. They are also beginning to form lifelong friendships and start going out without their parents for movies, sleepovers, and parties. Most of the money they have goes towards buying the right clothes, shoes, shaving creams, hair gels, shoes, or makeup.

This is the right time to have a discussion about budget formation as well as how they can grow their money by getting a job. It is time to teach them about the basics of income. They must know that they have to make the most of this time to find themselves a passion or career they wish to pursue and how to go about it. Talk about what it offers in terms of financial stability, how it will help them improve their existing skills, and what are the chances of progressing. Talk about the responsibilities they will have as they start planning to move out and how they are going to pay the bills when they do. Now will also be a good time to talk to them about how they will only be taking their basic salary home and have cuts in the form of taxes, insurance premiums, social security, etc.

In the same vein, talk to them about creating a personal budget so that they have a good amount saved up when they move out and get themselves a place. This way they won't have to worry about upfront payments that are usually paid to the landlord as a security deposit. If they keep a budget and save up, they won't have to ask you or their friends to pitch in or loan them some cash. Start by setting budgets for everyday things. How much will be spent on gas, food, or entertainment? All this must be discussed at home beforehand.

This is also the time to open a personal checking account. Teach them how to write a check and use the ATM using their debit card. If they are great savers and not compulsive spenders, this might also be a good time to open a savings account so that they can put in some money in it every month.

Also, give them a pep talk about credit cards and why they aren't always the best means. Most of them come with high-interest rates and fees which get deducted from the annual credit. Besides, if you know that your child will not be able to pay back, it is best to avoid getting them one as it will affect their credit score. If you must give them one, repeatedly remind them to not spend more than what they can afford or pay off each month.

The tuition fee for colleges these days is skyrocketing. You don't want your child to be buried under student debt. While they are young, compare the costs of tuition fees together and discuss how they are going to pay for college. Encourage them to start saving from now so that they have enough to pay off before they get a decent job and earn. If they are good at extracurricular, help them get a scholarship. Encourage them to start taking summer/spring/fall/winter jobs as they are going to need all the money that they can when they start college. Put that money in the savings account for now.

By the time they are 18, credit card companies will hound them with phone calls and lucrative offers. If they don't know any better, chances are they are going to fall for them. If you don't prepare them to avoid any risky or unwarranted decisions when you can, they will accumulate debt and that is a harmful way to begin their financial future. You don't want to raise another credit card victim. Moreover, now is the time to introduce them to compound interest and its benefits. You have to raise them as investment savvy. The sooner your teenager starts to invest, the better. We have a whole chapter dedicated to talking about investments and what avenues they can explore. Compound interest is interest on interest. You add interest on the principal amount of a deposit or a loan.

Then, talk to them about how they are going to make a living. What jobs are they applying for or planning to take up? Do they already have a place secured at a firm or store or are they going to start a new venture altogether and become an entrepreneur? Whichever is the case, they don't need to have a degree to start one as there are many money-earning ideas like babysitting, yard cleaning, or waitressing that don't require a degree. Your child can set up their business and attempt their luck on one of these in their spare time to make some money.

Activities

Although they are old enough to not fall for planned attempts, there are still some ways you can help them become financially literate and learn the value of money. To do this, you can give them a small budget project for a week or a month and see how well they fare. If they want to make an expensive purchase like get a new iPhone or go on a trip with their friends during the summers, promise to help them out with the expenses if they spend within the budget for a week. Ask them to research the best hotel deals and car rentals if they plan to go on a road trip before you give away the money. Discuss the best available options with them and then help them out. You can also sign them up for a temp job at a store or office to help them make money if you don't want to hand it to them. This way, they can earn it themselves and get what they have been dreaming of getting.

Then, there are many board games like Monopoly or Payday that you can play with your kids every weekend to see how well they are learning. Use game time to talk about how they are managing their allowance, what they are spending most, and how they can do better. This doesn't have to be a lecture but rather a subtle nudge to remind them that money is a scarce resource and doesn't grow on trees. Games like Payday put the player in many real-life financial situations where they have to be smart about their spending choices. The game takes the form of a monthly calendar where you get paid at the end of the month. The winner is someone with the most money at the end of the month. Payday is a great game if you want to teach your teen about the benefits of saving, making the right investments, and budgeting.

In Monopoly, teens learn a lot about delayed gratification and future planning. You start off buying properties to collect rents and making profits. It is the perfect game to talk about investments and their power.

Chapter 2:

Simple Money Concepts

Your Child Should Be

Aware of

Although much emphasis has already been made on teaching kids about basic money concepts, sometimes, it is the parents who need the schooling. Keep in mind, kids are visual learners. They do what they see others doing. Their parents are the first and most important interactions in their lives. If you don't have healthy money habits, you can't expect them to magically adopt them. If all they see is you fighting with your spouse about overspending and a lack of planning, they are going to assume it as a normalized behavior. If they see you falling behind on your bills every month, they are going to grow up thinking that it happens with everyone no matter what.

Set the right example for them to follow, especially when they are around. They shouldn't have to see you curse yourself for overspending on your credit card or have electricity cut because you failed to pay the bill. It all starts with you and how *you* handle your finances. You should be the epitome of perfection for them. Most of the learning will be done through your actions.

As for the rest of it, sometimes, when we do sit down with our kids to explain money basics, we have a hard time coming up with the right definition or example to explain them. This chapter covers the basics pretty well and has a financial glossary listing simple yet important financial terms that your child should be introduced to at an early age. Take a look!

Your Child's Very First Financial Glossary

Annual Return: It is the profit or loss on investment during one year.

ATM: An automated teller machine is a machine that allows bank customers to perform transactions such as withdrawals and deposits.

Bank: A bank is a financial institution that makes loans, accepts deposits, and handles other monetary transactions.

Borrow: To borrow money from either a financial institution or an individual means to take money from someone with the understanding that it shall be returned. When you borrow from a bank, it adds an interest rate along with some other charges, which increases the actual amount. A borrower is someone who borrows.

Budget: A budget is a plan outlining the money you have earned to be spent or saved in a given period of time. Creating a budget involves calculating all expenses that must be paid along with all the purchases you intend to perform. Going overboard means you failed to stay within the set limit.

Buying/purchasing power: Buying power is the number of goods and services that can be purchased taking into account inflation by any given unit of currency.

Checking account: A checking account is a basic account opened in a bank that allows you to make deposits, withdrawals, and pay bills.

Commission: Commission is the additional earning you receive when you sell something. Brokers and salespeople work on a commission most of the time.

Credit: Credit means borrowing money or the right to borrow money to buy something. A credit card allows you to buy the stuff you want to without having to pay right away. You borrow the money from the credit card's bank and then, every month pay some of it off. It comes with interest rates and is like a loan.

Credit card: To be more specific, a credit card is an open-ended loan where you borrow money up to a certain limit. You carry an unpaid balance from one month to another. You continue to make minimum payments each month and thus, there is no fixed time for repayment.

Credit limit: A limit on the credit card is set by the credit card company on what amount of money you can use on it. Once the limit is reached, you have to repay some of the loan to be able to use it again.

Credit score: Your credit score is a number created by mathematical formulas. It tracks and analyzes your credit history to calculate a score. A good credit rating helps you get loans faster and makes you a trustworthy individual.

Debit card: It is a plastic card that can be used to make transactions on purchases and the money gets deducted from your checking account. It is an alternative for cold cash.

Debt: A debt is a sum of money that you owe someone or a business.

Earned Income: Earned income is the amount of money you earn by working a job. If you are in business, it is the profits you have earned. It also includes all the tips, wages, and income you receive from working.

Exchange Rate: An exchange rate is a number used to compare the money value of different currencies.

Fixed expenses: Fixed expenses are bills that must be paid each month like the electricity and gas bill. As you use the commodity every day, you have to pay the price.

Identity theft: An identity theft is when someone steals your personal information like your name, credit card, or social security number without permission and uses it.

Inflation: Inflation means that the prices of services and goods have risen over time. The higher the inflation rate, the more expensive things get.

Insurance: Insurance is a form of arrangement that the government or a private company provides to its buyers. It guarantees compensation for damage, loss, illness, or death.

Interest: Interest is a fee charged by financial institutions and lenders for the use of money.

Interest rate: The interest rate is the percentage of the sum borrowed by the lender or an institution for using its money. A 5% interest rate means you will have to pay an additional 5% on the total amount you owe the lender.

Investment: An investment is anything you spend your money on and hope for a profitable financial return.

Liability: A liability is a disadvantage, debt, or money owed, as per the law.

Loan: A loan is the amount of money borrowed from a lending company/individual and must be repaid, generally with interest.

Mortgage: Mortgage is a legal agreement in which a bank or building society lends an individual or firm money at interest in exchange for the debtor's property title. If the borrower fails to make payments, the title will become void.

Needs: Needs are essentials that you require to survive. These include food, shelter, clothing, etc.

Online banking: Online banking is a service that enables you to use a secure website and manage your finances without the aid of a teller. You can send and receive money or transfer money between different accounts on your own.

Opportunity cost: When you choose one alternative over the other, you incur an opportunity cost. Think of it as the next best use of your time or money.

Out-of-pocket cost: This is the cost that no insurance company reimburses. This includes deductibles, amounts paid for repairs or services, and copayments that are excluded from coverage.

Savings: Your savings is the money you have set aside. It is usually stored in a saving account and used for future purchases or emergencies.

Savings account: A savings account is another type of bank account where you set aside money for later use.

Most saving accounts provide you interest rates, meaning your money grows.

Taxes: Taxes are the sums of money paid to the government, which are then used for the welfare of the citizens. The government uses the collected funds to provide public goods, build parks, roads, and recreational spots.

Wants: Wants are upgrades that are nice to have but not necessary for living.

Chapter 3:

Creating Opportunities to

Earn Money

Children of all ages learn about money and its many uses from their parents. However, learning about it isn't enough. They need to implement and adopt good money habits too, especially when they are of an age where they begin to seek part-time job opportunities.

When your children enter their teens, many tempting money-making opportunities will come their way. They will be eager to earn because something is pleasing about getting paid. Some kids have it easy when it comes to finding a job. They have their peers or friends helping them out. Their parents hire their own kids to work with them in their business or workplace. For others, it's a bit difficult.

This is where your suggestions and encouragement come in. Sit down with them and talk about what interests your child the most. Then, together, find something suitable that is related to their interests and help them get started. For example, if your teen is into baking, you can help them come up with a brand name, print labels for boxes, and have them sell their freshly-baked delicacies in the neighborhood or at a nearby local bakery. If they aren't shy, you can even set up a YouTube channel for them where they upload recipes and hacks that make them an amazing baker. As the viewership and subscribers grow, they can start to monetize it and earn a living from it.

This is just one of the many ideas to earn money for kids. Many others are listed below.

Baby Sitting

Among teens, babysitting is a common and popular choice. As both parents work to make the ends meet, young kids are often left under the supervision of babysitters. If you are comfortable having them stay at someone else's home and look after their child, this can be a productive way to pass time, earn money, and learn about responsibility.

House cleaning

If you don't like the idea of them spending time at someone's house, you can pay them for chores inside the house. You can create a list of all the chores that need to be done like mowing the lawn, watering the plants, vacuuming, dusting, feeding the pets, cleaning the kitchen or bathroom, and so on and pay them for the services. To keep it fair, you can offer them market-competitive incentives so that they don't feel like they are being scammed by their parents.

Parents' helper

A parent helper is similar to that of a babysitter except that the parent also stays in the house. Some mothers with multiple kids require additional assistance to look after their kids. Women who have more than one kid under the age of five will have a hard time attending to them. Your child can assist by offering to play with the other kid(s) while the parent feeds one or they can help put the younger siblings down for a nap. Your child can also help them take a bath, help with the chores, and tutor the school-aged kids.

Lemonade Stand

A lemonade stand in the heat of summer is a great money-generating idea. It gives the kids something to do and a way to earn through their hard work. Help your child set up a stand in the front of the house, gather the supplies they would need, and keep a register of all the sales made. If the stand or cart is mobile, you can even take it to a park nearby and give your child more exposure and opportunity to make money.

Crafts Seller

A lemonade stand isn't the only booth that your child can create. Many communities put on a yearly fair where everyone gets a chance to engage, interact, and communicate. If your child is particularly good at arts and crafts, tell them that they can make money off of it by setting up a stall at the fair. You can help them come up with new designs and ideas using sites like Pinterest, Etsy, and YouTube.

Car Washing

This is yet another seasonal but popular money-generating business ideas for teenagers. Your child can gather a few of their friends, get some car washing equipment or rent and start their own car washing business in your garage. As the car owners wait for their cars to be washed, you can sell them some drinks or better, homemade, freshly-squeezed lemonade.

Animal Caretaker

If your child loves pets, you can suggest walking dogs or caring for other people's pets in some way. If they enjoy doing so and the pet owners seem happy with their job, encourage your child to expand their services to washing or grooming the pets, too.

Pet Sitting

Like babysitting, your child can also take care of people's pets when they are out for work or go on vacations or business trips. You can look after their food, clean after them, and walk them. You can charge additional fees if your child also decides to look after the house, water the plants, and vacuum.

Landscaping Services

Every season comes with its own unique challenge when gardening. The grass needs to be cut, weed needs to be pulled out, plants must be watered, and bushes need to be trimmed. If you can rent out the equipment, you can ask your child to search for homes that require landscaping services and offer to help out at a reasonable rate.

Snow Removal

During the winters, your child can also volunteer to clear the snow from driveways and sidewalks using a shovel. Your kid can team up with a couple of other kids and start a small business. In autumn, your small business can offer services like raking the leaves and cleaning the gardens.

Yard or Garage Sales

You and your child can set up a yard sale where you give away old clothes, furniture, paintings, lamps, carpets, or anything else cluttering up the house that are no longer needed or have been stored away in the storeroom for long. Your child can create cartons of old clothes, shoes, toys, and books that they will no longer be needing and earn a respectable amount from them.

Get an Internship

If you are an entrepreneur or businessman, you can hire your kid to work for you and perform simple tasks like make tea, shred mail, type replies for you, Xerox documents, get supplies from the shop, or drive the final product to the wholesalers and resellers. But before that, make sure they have earned their driving license fair and square!

Write Stories or Poems

If they are interested in literature and have a knack for writing poems, lyrics, or short stories, encourage them

photography services for small events like birthday parties, engagement shoots, or weddings.

They can also take online surveys and earn money by answering simple questions. However, ensure that you are aware of the kind of surveys they are opting to be a part of. Some surveys take less than five minutes to complete. They can also enter focus group studies and write product reviews or testimonials for websites.

If they are good at graphic or logo designing or are exceptional writers, they can also set up a free account on sites like Upwork, Freelancer, or Guru to find work. There are tons of projects listed every day that pay well. If your children are good with researching, they can find something of their interest and make fast money writing from the comfort of home.

They can also start a blog and talk about some social issue or topic of their interest. If they love to write scripts, short stories, or novellas, they can easily create a fan base by posting their stories on their blog. Starting early, however, is the key here. By the time they can handle the account themselves, you can help them out and aid them in reaching the point of monetization by getting people to subscribe to their blog.

If they have old stuff lying around, they can also make money off of it by listing it on websites like Craigslist, Facebook Marketplace, or eBay Classifieds.

Your child can also set up a YouTube channel where they can talk about a ton of important stuff. YouTube is a decent and user-friendly website that offers great monetization opportunities. The genres are endless. Kids can share recipes, talk about different products and review them, watch trailers and react to them, discuss religion, or give sports reviews on the latest games. If they are great with marketing, they can review products for their followers. They can also earn sponsorships if they have a decent following. They can even create vlogs where they tell their followers how they spend their days, or weekends and place ads in the beginning to generate income.

Chapter 4:

A Penny Saved Is a Penny

Earned

As adults, we are more experienced in handling finances than our children. We are weathered to the world and we know the importance of saving for a rainy day. We have had friends who were desperate to borrow from others because their expenses were greater than their income and we never want our kids to go through the same. When teaching our children about finances, saving money is another important building block. It secures their future and prevents them from going bankrupt. We can't rely solely on the schools to encourage savings. We have to get them on board and preach the habit ourselves.

In this chapter, we look at how we can empower our kids to learn the importance of saving. Even if you are from a secure or wealthy family, teaching them how to save is imperative so that they don't end up making unnecessary and wasteful purchases in the future.

How to Save 101

First off, it's crucial to have the concept of saving well-engraved in your children's minds. They shouldn't feel forced to save but rather keen to do so. Talk with them about the many benefits of saving from an early age and about investing that money to watch it grow. Make them aware of the many long-term goals they can fulfill if they put merely $10 in a savings account every month.

Provide them with a place to save. This can be a jar, piggy bank, or a checking account. The goal is to have a designated place to stash their cash with saving in mind. Be sure to tell them to place it somewhere where they can view it every day. Count the money they have saved every week and praise your little saver for doing so. Promise to add a bit from your pocket if they reach a certain saving goal so that they can see their money grow over time.

Track the Spending

To save, you must have something to set aside. This calls for expenditure analysis. It doesn't have to be a lecturing session where you make your child feel demotivated if they have done poorly. The idea is to encourage tracking to see where most of their money is going and whether what they are spending on is a need or a want. Have them write down all the purchases they made in a day—each day—so that they can learn to cut down where possible. For example, if the majority of their allowance is being spent on a want you can offer encouragement and remind them that they will reach their long-term goals faster if they hold back and only spend on what's necessary. This will help shift their spending patterns and cut down on frivolous expenditures. This means more money in the savings jar at the end of the day.

Offer Incentives

We all love free money and your teenager is no different. Just like most companies offer their employees retirement plans where they can save a fraction of their income to not end up empty-handed, you can do the same for your teenager. Offer them incentives they can't resist, especially if you are having trouble motivating them to save. If they have a long-term goal like buying a PlayStation, make a deal to offer a fraction of their total saved money every time they reach a certain milestone. For example, if something they need costs $500 and they have saved $100, tell them that you will offer a bonus of $25 for doing so. They can expect to receive the same when they reach $200 and then $300.

Act as a Creditor

A creditor is someone you owe money to. If your child is being impatient about something they want, you can lend to them for now as long as they return it with a 5% interest. Set a timeline and tell them that if they aren't able to pay back before that, the interest rate will increase. This will not only make them eager to save and give back the borrowed money, but it will also get the conversation about interest going. Here, also talk to them about how delayed gratification means buying something for less.

Use Savings Jars

If your child is young and has their eye on something expensive like a new action figure or a toy car, tell them that they will have to save up for it. Start by giving them an allowance and set up a savings jar. To encourage saving, stick a picture of the thing that they long to have on the jar so that they feel motivated. Also, when giving money, don't hand out a $5 bill. Break it into $1 each so that they can put some of it right away in the savings jar.

Gift a Piggy Bank

If your child is less than five, a piggy bank might tempt them to develop the habit of saving. If you have more than one kid, get each of them a piggy bank of their own and tell them that whoever fills up their piggy bank first with dollars and coins will win and receive something of their choice. Once the piggy bank fills up, take them to their favorite shop, and let them buy something using the money that they saved. This will make them feel proud of themselves and they'll become lifelong savers. To further motivate, set up milestones and celebrate whenever your child reaches one. For example, if they had to save $5 per week and they achieved that goal, reward them, so that they continue with the same behavior.

Set up a Timeline

For young ones, the concept of time and money is a hard one to grasp. They are soon to forget all about what they have learned if they aren't provided the right opportunities to implement the teachings. To ensure that the message sticks, make money lessons a weekly or monthly ritual. If they are expected to receive cash on their birthday, sit down with them and talk about budgeting before they get it.

Create timelines for both long-term and short-term goals so that your child is reminded constantly of them. For example, if they want to buy something that costs $50 and you give them an allowance of $5 each week, they will reach their goal on the tenth week, given that they saved up all of their allowances. However, since this isn't possible in most cases, set up smaller saving milestones that they can reach. Take a pen and paper and plan how they are going to save each week and then calculate how many weeks it will take to get there. Place it somewhere highly visible so that they stay motivated. Each week, mark how much your child has saved, and how much more they must to reach their end goal. Chances are, they'll strive to reach the end goal sooner and save more than what was initially settled upon.

Benefits of Having a Savings Account

If your kids are of an age where they already have a checking account and are earning via part-time gigs, have them set up a savings account too. Savings accounts are a lot like a checking account, except they come with opportunities to grow your money in the long run as they offer a chance to earn interest. Checking accounts are more apt for everyday transactions. In a savings account, you stash cash and then forget about it. Some experts believe that setting up a savings account for a child as little as five is one of the most sensible things a parent can do because a decade and a half down the line, they might already have enough to get themselves a place to live in. Other benefits include:

Getting kids in the money game. When we were young, most of our learning about finances came from our experiences at the nearest corner shop where we went to buy candy from what we had saved. However, children are not going to stores as often, as they have the luxury to order everything in. This prevents kids from learning about money and how it can be saved. A savings account is a big step to teach them about it and paves the way for money conversations, keeping the little ones intrigued about how their money is growing.

Savings accounts develop healthy money-saving habits. Having a savings account is the key to financial security but your teen may not understand the value, yet. However, if you make them save up every month and stash it in the savings account, over time, they will develop the habit to do so. Start early by encouraging them to save some of their allowances or earn more money by doing part-time gigs.

It can help children of all ages learn what savings are all about. You can do so by incentivizing it or matching it. Every time your child adds something to the savings account, you add the same amount or a percentage of it on your behalf so that they can see their money grow. This will greatly help them when they are on their own and trying to make a living independently.

Your children can use their saved money to help with their college funds and other finances like buying a car or getting a place for themselves. If they have student loans, they can use that money to pay them off and still have more to spend at the end of the day.

Introduce them to the concept of investing. Once they are into saving, you can gradually shift their focus from savings to investing in mutual funds and stocks. You can also help them learn how to use different banking apps and understand various relevant terms and conditions. As your kids get older, they can invest their saved money into other money-making projects and double their earnings. By the time they are an adult, they might have enough to start a business or pay the mortgage.

Having a savings account will help them set long-term financial goals and make the right decisions. They will learn to value money and spend it wisely.

The Right Age to Open a Savings Account

There is no right age to start saving. Your child should already be saving as a tot. Of course, then, they are too young to set up a savings account for themselves which is why you need to step in. Open a savings account with joint ownership. Your child can become the sole owner of it when they turn 18. Until then, you can manage the finances and keep a track of all the additional money you make on it. However, there is no rush to do so if you are confident that you are instilling some good money values in them.

Ideally, when researching for a savings account, your best bet is to find a bank that:

- Requires no minimum balance or monthly maintenance fee. Your child will be disheartened if they see their savings being reduced every month when you promised that it would grow.
- Promises an above-average interest rate. In most national bank settings, the interest rates hover around 0.4% but there are some credit unions and online banks that give better rates. The more interest you earn, the sooner your money will grow, and the more delighted your little one will be!

- Has easy online access. It is rather bothersome to wait for a bi-annual statement. Any bank or credit union that offers easy access to bank statements, transaction history, and interest earnings online is better. Although most banks now have mobile apps that offer this feature, be sure to go with the right one. You can get your kid to set up a password of their liking and learn to surf the internet safely.

Chapter 5:

Budgeting for Kids – How to Become Wise Spenders

Budgeting is such a simple concept yet most people can't live by it. It is difficult to put it into practice. We all know the basics and still, we don't follow our budget diligently. This is the harsh reality. Most people, despite knowing its importance, don't thrive to create one as per these statistics . The world of digital media makes it so easy with tons of basic apps and online budgeting templates but only a mere 32% of America's population believes in creating budgets and following them regularly (*Personal finance statistics*, 2019).

If we can't stick to a budget, how can we expect our kids to do the same? If they see us going overboard and using money from our savings account to pitch in for the bills, they will learn to do the same. To encourage them to build wealth and save some for the future, they need to know the basics of creating a budget and sticking to it.

Creating a budget is simple. You need to break the whole process into five simple steps.

1. Keep track of your income and expenses every month.
2. Create different categories for different types of needs.
3. Cut down expenses that can be saved.
4. Set short-term and long-term goals.
5. Adjust the budget every month or week to meet the requirements.

There are always some unexpected expenses that can kill the budget, which is why the last step is the most crucial. There is always a chance that things won't go as planned and unexpected expenses will creep up. However, this requires a re-assessment of needs and not borrowing money from others or sneaking some from the savings account.

If you go overboard with some important expenses, ensure to stay within the set parameters next time. These are some of the many things that your kids must know before they start building themselves a budget. Below are some fun and entertaining activities that will help you discuss setting a budget with your kids. They are simple and action-oriented, sure to develop a healthy budgeting habit.

Fun Activities to Teach Children About the Perks of Budgeting

We will start with the most basic and that is "three jars budgeting." As the name suggests, you will need three jars. Label the empty jars as follows: savings, spending, and the third, sharing. Every time your child receives an allowance or money as a gift, ask them to place some of it in all three jars. It is up to them to decide in which jar they want to put the most. If they want to buy something right away, they can put most of it in the spending jar and use it the next hour. If they have a long-term goal in mind, they might want to put more in the savings jar to fill it up all the way and vice versa. This is them budgeting their money without even knowing that they are.

The third jar, which is for sharing accumulates the amount your child wishes to give away to help the poor. To motivate them to do so, let them decide which charitable organization or person they wish to give it to. For example, they might want to use it to bake cookies for the needy on the street or buy the garbage man a gift of appreciation. If they go to church, they can put that money in the collection bucket. If they want to free captured animals or buy food for the dogs at the shelter, they can do that as well! If you empower them to choose on their own, they will feel happier helping.

DIY Budgeting Game

This is an exciting game to play with your kid(s). Give them a budget to begin with. Then bring in some challenges and unexpected expenses like getting fined with a ticket, paying for a tire change, or saving for a last minute trip with their friends over the weekend. Create different budgeting categories depending on what they mostly spend on and see which ones they can cut to make room for the added expenditures. Whichever participant ends with the most money at the end of the activity wins.

Your Child's Savings First-Aid Kit

In this activity, you and your little one start with a set amount for a month. Then, you brainstorm possible unexpected expenditures that occur in life and decide how you will make space for them by cutting back on your normal expenses. An unexpected expense can be a school trip, a nose bleed that requires medical care or supplies, or additional money for school accessories.

It is simple but effective as it encourages kids to brainstorm and problem-solve with the limited options they have.

The Bean Game

This doesn't involve real money but rather 20 beans that you give your child at the start of the game. Tell them that each bean equates to $1 and then present them with a list of items and categories that they will have to spend the beans on. Make some categories as musts so that your child will have to spend at least one or two of their beans, leaving them with little for the other categories. Every time you play the game, you can reduce the number of beans so that your child has to strategize and make wiser decisions. At the end of the game, ask them why they spent a certain number of beans in one category and why they left the others out.

Chapter 6:

Making Money Grow –

Investments

Many would say investing is the first step, but we believe it is the finish line. Before getting into complex money discussions with your child, make it clear to them that some money is for now and some is for later. We've already covered saving, so now we are going to focus on investing. The reason kids are drawn to the spending, saving, and sharing jars is because it helps them understand the concept of delayed gratification visually.

Now that your child is a teenager, they must be taught that not every penny earned must be spent. They must be introduced to the idea that if they have patience, they can watch their money grow with time. The first few paychecks that roll in as they start to work serve the best opportunity to get them interested in the idea of investments and mutual funds.

Investing is complex and risky. But if you are smart about where you invest, it doesn't have to be. Even the most successful of billionaires started with nothing, just like your teen. However, the reason they build empires and gather fortunes is due to smart investments. Read about any successful entrepreneur's journey and you will learn that one of the many ways they were able to double and triple their income is through smart investments at the right time. Of course, we don't expect your teen to become a billionaire hedge fund manager when they turn 21, but , nonetheless, now is the time to start talking about investments.

How to Talk Investments With Kids

When having a conversation about investments with your teenager, there are a few things you must keep in mind.

Although investments can be chancy, keep the conversation around investments positive. Highlight the positive aspects and talk repeatedly about the benefits they can yield. At this age, they will need a compelling reason not to get their car a new paint job and save their money. As they are earning, they will want to spend their money their way, which is why you must not try to impose any financial decisions on them. Keep the conversation simple, positive, and uplifting. Show them the benefits using real-life examples of stock market billionaires who earned their way to the top.

Find the right time to have the conversation. Take advantage of the time when they are alone with you like on a drive to school, grocery shopping, or on a doctor's visit. Present them with evidence and facts to get them interested. Give them small researching tasks to intrigue them. Make sure they are well-informed about how the market works and what is in it for them. Be open to answering any questions they might have, no matter how seemingly silly they are.

Label different services and appliances that you use in the house and talk about the companies that provide them. Then, ask them to research if those companies offer shares to purchase and at what costs. The companies they will be interested in will become their target companies. For a few months, track the company's share progress and decide if it is a share worth investing in or not.

Let them know that investing is about the long term. It isn't like they will earn the benefits the next day. They will have to incur some losses too but that is okay. Most investors adopt the principle of "buy and hold." They invest the money they don't need in the short term. Talk to them about stock market billionaires like Peter Lynch and Warren Buffett.

Let them make mistakes. Let them feel some losses by investing a small sum of money. Making mistakes will teach them not to repeat the same blunders and master the art of investing.

Teenagers and Investing

CNBC's Mad Money host, Jim Cramer believes that with a 10% annual return, investors can double their money in about seven years. Now imagine how much your young adult would have when they finish college and decide to get a job. Heck, they might not even need one, if given the right guidance on how to enter the stock market and invest in shares.

Many people believe that investing is a risky business. True, but it is also one that can make you lots of money. Imagine your child put away 10% of their birthday cash, side job money, or allowance they receive from you for investment. To promote the habit and develop an understanding, do the following activity with them.

Ask them if they had three buckets, one for spending, one for donation, and one for investing, each filled with water, which one would they want to fill first? Let them think and present their answer. If they choose the first two, and then the third, tell them that the first two buckets are placed in the sun and lose water every minute through evaporation. Ask them what strategies they will apply to save as much water as possible. They might suggest covering it up with a lid or placing it away from the sun.

Now is the time to give them some true wisdom. The reason the first two buckets will keep losing water is that unexpected expenses can occur any day at any time and there is only so much that we can do about it. Even the money in the savings account loses value because of inflation over time.

Bucket number 3 sits on a rain gutter and rain droplets trickle into the bucket, filling it. It will continue to fill up until water starts to pour out. They should, therefore, prioritize filling the third bucket first because it can help them fill the other buckets too when the water evaporates.

Let Them Dip Their Feet

To introduce your teenager to the stock world, let them dip their feet in the game. Unless they see for themselves how their money grows, they will be less likely to invest. Motivate your teen to use real money and invest in a share of their choice. This is the only way to keep vested interest. Ask them to see how the share values fluctuate with time and create a pattern to invest in the right shares.

Open a High-Yield Savings Account

We have already discussed this earlier in Chapter 4 but it must be stressed because of the great benefits a high-yield savings account offers.

Although investing in stocks is a good bet, it isn't wise to invest all of your money into the stock market. You must keep some of it in a savings account and watch it grow, thanks to the high-interest rates. As teens are tech-savvy, they shouldn't have a problem researching online banks and credit unions that offer high-interest rates. Savings accounts are there to build the habit of saving.

Open a Roth IRA

For a teenager, it might be hard to imagine themselves retiring because they are just spreading their wings to fly away but it is the reality. They should know the importance of saving and investing in the right mediums so that they can build wealth that will help them when they retire. One of the best ways is for them to open a Roth IRA. Investments in the Roth IRA grow tax-free as long as you wait until you are fifty-nine to withdraw. Simply tell them to invest in it and forget about it.

Buy a Stock

Any stock will do as long as the teenager understands its importance and value. Investing in stocks can be a great learning experience for teenagers. They can pick ones that they are familiar with or prefer and see them grow with time. Over time, they can sense how the market works and what different stocks they can invest in. The more engaged they are, the sooner they will pick up the tricks and double their initial money in no time. They will become more trained to predict market trends, research the companies they plan to invest in, and build resilience when they receive a minor setback.

If your teenager seems interested but would like to hear from the experts themselves, there is this amazing podcast called *Pounding The Table* by two guys Anthony Ohayon and Avi Mash who talk about how to start in the stock market world, which market trends to follow, and how to earn peak profits in a simple yet convincing manner.

Conclusion

Financial literacy should begin at an early age. The benefits outnumber the reasons you keep giving yourselves that they are too naive to take in the money talks right now. Surely, you want to raise them as smart, money-savvy, and financially independent. We know through research that a child's money habits are formed by the time they turn seven. This means that if they don't get the basics right by then, they never might.

This brief guide has helped you accomplish that goal of making them financially literate by covering topics, such as what age-appropriate activities are suitable for kids and teens. It talks about how they can spend wisely, save for a rainy day, and invest their money into stocks and mutual funds so that they may reap the benefits later on. If you stick with the activities and exercises discussed in this book, you can raise your children to become financially independent by the time they are adults.

Thank you for giving this book a read. I hope you loved reading it as much as I enjoyed writing it. It would make me the happiest person on earth if you would take a moment to leave an honest review. All you have to do is visit the site where you purchased this book: It's that simple! The review doesn't have to be a full-fledged paragraph; a few words will do. Your few words will help others decide if this is what they should be reading as well. Thank you in advance, and best of luck with your parenting adventures. Every moment is a joyous one with a child.

References

15 ways to teach kids about money. (2021, February 25). Ramsey Solutions. https://www.ramseysolutions.com/relationships/how-to-teach-kids-about-money

Attkisson, A. (2021, March 31). *Teaching kids about money: An age-by-age guide.* Parents. https://www.parents.com/parenting/money/family-finances/teaching-kids-about-money-an-age-by-age-guide/

Benefits of financial literacy for kids. (2016, October 14). Campbellsville University Online Programs. https://online.campbellsville.edu/education/financial-literacy-for-kids/

Booth, B. (2020, January 29). *It's not just about saving. teach your teen to invest now to set them up for a financially healthy life.* CNBC. https://www.cnbc.com/2020/01/29/teaching-teenagers-to-invest-now-will-set-them-up-for-life.html

Bruce, K. (2019, July 30). *Budgeting for kids: How to teach budgeting from age 3 to 18*. Freedom Sprout. https://freedomsprout.com/budgeting-for-kids/

Field, B. (n.d.). *Financial literacy for kids: Top 8 lessons, activities & delivery tips*. NFEC. Retrieved April 26, 2021, from https://www.financialeducatorscouncil.org/financial-literacy-for-kids/#:~:text=The%20Importance%20Of%20Financial%20Literacy

Financial terms glossary. (n.d.). Consumer Financial Protection Bureau. Retrieved April 30, 2021, from https://www.consumerfinance.gov/consumer-tools/educator-tools/youth-financial-education/glossary/

Gobler, E. (2020, November 7). *The best investments for teens and how to start*. Clever Girl

Finance.
https://www.clevergirlfinance.com/blog/invest
ments-for-teens/

Grossman, A. L. (2019, November 25). *12 fun budgeting activities pdfs for students (kids & teens).* Money Prodigy.
https://www.moneyprodigy.com/fun-budgeting-activities-pdfs/

How are teens spending money? (2017, October 19). Marketing Charts.
https://www.marketingcharts.com/demographics-and-audiences-80708

How to teach kids about money at every age. (2019, December 12). MoneyGeek.com.
https://www.moneygeek.com/financial-planning/resources/how-to-teach-your-kids-about-money/

Kadlec, D. (2014, April 16). Turns out millennials are scary smart with their money. Time. https://time.com/64137/millennials-money/

Lake, R. (2021, March). *10 tips to teach your children to save money*. Investopedia. https://www.investopedia.com/personal-finance/10-tips-teach-your-child-save/

Lemke, T. (2020, September 19). *What teens need to know to start investing*. The Balance. https://www.thebalance.com/investing-guide-for-teens-and-parents-4588018

Let's learn about money! Teaching young children about money (better kid care). (n.d.). Better Kid Care (Penn State Extension). https://extension.psu.edu/programs/betterkidcare/knowledge-areas/environment-curriculum/activities/all-activities/let2019s-learn-about-money-teaching-young-children-about-money

Lusardi, A., & Mitchell, O. S. (2014). The economic importance of financial literacy: Theory and evidence. Journal of Economic Literature, 52(1), 5–44. https://doi.org/10.1257/jel.52.1.5

Mavor, A. (2019, November 27). *Investing for teens: The beginner's guide - wealthfit.* Https://Wealthfit.com. https://wealthfit.com/articles/investing-for-teens/

Meleen, M. (2018). *Teen consumer spending habits.* LoveToKnow; LoveToKnow Corp. https://teens.lovetoknow.com/Teen_Consumer_Spending_Habits

Montanaro, J. J. (n.d.). *Five reasons all kids should have savings accounts.* The American Legion. Retrieved April 30, 2021, from https://www.legion.org/magazine/234121/five-reasons-all-kids-should-have-savings-accounts

O'Connell, B. (2017, August 25). *Here are 5 tips for talking to teens about stocks and wealth creation.* TheStreet. https://www.thestreet.com/personal-finance/here-are-5-tips-for-talking-to-teens-about-stocks-and-wealth-creation-14284006

Pant, P. (2018, November 18). *Teach your kids to budget money*. The Balance. https://www.thebalance.com/teach-kids-to-budget-money-454012

Pearl, J. A. (1999). *Kids and money : Giving them the savvy to succeed financially*. Bloomberg Press.

Pearl, M. (2017, September 19). *How to teach kids about money, from toddlers to teens*. The Simple Dollar. https://www.thesimpledollar.com/financial-wellness/how-to-teach-kids-about-money-from-toddlers-to-teens/

Personal finance statistics. (2019). Debt.com; Debt.com, LLC. https://www.debt.com/statistics/

Pounding the table. (2021, February 10). https://poundingthetablepodcast.com/.

Six ways to teach your kids about saving money. (2015, October 15). Windgate Wealth Management.

https://windgatewealth.com/six-ways-to-teach-your-kids-about-saving-money/

Swanbrow, D. (2014). *How teen workers spend their money: U-M study shows trends.* Institute for Social Research. https://isr.umich.edu/news-events/news-releases/how-teen-workers-spend-their-money-um-study-shows-trends/

Thukral, A. (2019, October 28). *Why it's important to make your children financially literate.* The Financial Express. https://www.financialexpress.com/money/why-its-important-to-make-your-children-financially-literate/1747571/

Tierney, S. (2021, February 19). *Kids savings accounts: What you need to know.* NerdWallet. https://www.nerdwallet.com/article/banking/opening-child-first-bank-account

Ways for kids to make money – money instructor. (n.d.). Money Instructor. http://content.moneyinstructor.com/656/ways-kids-make-money.html

Weltman, A. (n.d.). *How your child spends his allowance - familyeducation.* Www.familyeducation.com. https://www.familyeducation.com/life/allowance/how-your-child-spends-his-allowance

Why is financial literacy important for children? (2020, October 29). Www.indiainfoline.com. https://www.indiainfoline.com/article/financial-literacy-explained/why-is-financial-literacy-important-for-children-120102900770_1.html

Williams, G. (2021). *Fun ways to teach kids about money.* US News & World Report; U.S. News & World Report. https://money.usnews.com/money/personal-finance/family-finance/articles/ways-to-teach-kids-about-money

www.ingramcontent.com/pod-product-compliance
Lightning Source LLC
LaVergne TN
LVHW051427080426
835508LV00022B/3272